VICTORIA & ALBERT MUSEUM

THEATRE POSTERS

Catherine Haill

Theatre Museum, V&A

LONDON: HER MAJESTY'S STATIONERY OFFICE

© Crown copyright 1983
First published 1983
Photography by Graham Brandon

ISBN 0 11 290418 1

HER MAJESTY'S STATIONERY OFFICE
Government Bookshops
49 High Holborn, London WC1V 6HB
13a Castle Street, Edinburgh EH2 3AR
Brazennose Street, Manchester M60 8AS
Southey House, Wine Street, Bristol BS1 2BQ
258 Broad Street, Birmingham B1 2HE
80 Chichester Street, Belfast BT1 4JY
*Government Publications are also available
through booksellers*
The full range of Museum publications
is displayed and sold at the
Victoria and Albert Museum
South Kensington
London SW7 2RL
Obtainable in the USA and Canada from the
Kraus-Thomson Organisation Ltd
Millwood
New York 10546
USA

FRONT COVER *A London Street Scene* View of a poster hoarding near St. Paul's Cathedral. Oil painting by John Parry, 1840. Reproduced by courtesy of Alfred Dunhill Ltd.

BACK COVER *Boardie Willie*. Photograph by Frank Meadow Sutcliffe. Reproduced by courtesy of the Sutcliffe Gallery, Whitby, Yorkshire.

Printed in the UK for HMSO
Dd 718114 C60

THEATRE POSTERS

Every live performance needs an audience, and some form of advertising has always been necessary to attract spectators. Mediaeval plays, acted by guildsmen on movable stages or in small outdoor arenas, were heralded by the performers themselves, often with the accompaniment of drum-beating and music. After the excitement caused by this announcement to those present, the news of the impending performance would quickly spread by word of mouth. By 1558, when Elizabeth came to the throne, religious drama was waning, mainly as a result of the Reformation, and the acting profession was considered decidedly disreputable. The only public performances were farcical interludes and tumbling, and other acrobatic feats, that occurred in places such as inn-yards. These would have been announced by the actors themselves, but for the literate a few details of the performance were hand-written and stuck on street posts around the town. From this practice the word poster originates, and in a letter of 1564—the year Shakespeare was born—the Bishop of London complained bitterly about this custom, railing against:

> 'these Histriones, common playours, who now daylye, but specially on holydayes, set up bills, wherunto the youthe resorteth excessively.'

In 1576, shortly after acting was officially recognised as a legitimate profession (if patronised by a peer of the realm), James Burbage of the Earl of Leicester's Company, opened the first public theatre in London, simply called The Theatre. The Curtain theatre followed a year later, and performances at both theatres were announced by the distribution and posting of hand-bills, as well as by flag-hoisting at the theatres and probably a drum procession throughout the streets a few hours before the performance. Immediately before the play began, a trumpeter standing in the cock-loft of the theatre gave three trumpet calls, a practice which is referred to bitterly by the priest John Stockwood in a sermon of 1578:

> 'Wyll not a fylthye play, with the blast of a Trumpette, sooner call thyther a thousande, than an houres tolling of a Bell, bring to the sermon a hundred?'

The earliest bills, probably measuring about 7" × 3", would have given only the briefest details about the play. By 1587 we know that some of them were printed, since one John Charlewood was in October that year granted a licence for 'the only ympryntinge of all manner of bills for players.' But just as the practice of flag-hoisting at theatres continued in Restoration days at the end of the 17th century, so hand-written playbills would have persisted as well as the printed ones, particularly in country areas. Those that were printed were produced on hand-made, laid rag paper, using the relief method known as letterpress in which letterforms cut in reverse were inked and printed on a wooden hand-press. Most ephemeral text was produced this way, while more delicate prints such as maps and book-plates, were produced by copper engraving. In this intaglio process, the ink was retained in the engraved lines when the surface of the plate was wiped clean of ink, and forced onto the paper when printed under pressure. Both processes stemmed from the 15th century, but letterpress remained the basic method for the playbill printer well into the 19th century.

Public theatrical performances were forbidden during the Puritan interregnum, 1642-1660, although surreptitious performances still took place, privately advertised. After the Restoration of Charles II, however, public theatre flourished again and the custom of posting bills openly also recommenced. That inveterate theatre-goer Samuel Pepys records looking for playbills on 24 March 1662:

> 'I went to see if any play was acted, and I found none upon the post, it being Passion week.'

As in Elizabethan days, the earliest Restoration playbills would have been small, and would have contained only the date (but not the year), the name of the theatre, the title of the play, the starting time and whether it was a new piece or a revival. They were stuck on posts and fences, distributed in the town particularly in coffee-houses and inns, and delivered to the homes of wealthy theatre-goers. The development of larger-sized bills or posters seems to have been influenced by a visit to London in 1672 of a French theatre Company, who brought with them larger bills printed in red lettering. The poet and dramatist John Dryden (1631-1700) records this innovation in his prologue to Carlwell's play *Arviragus and Philicia* which was acted at Lincoln's Inn Fields, Easter 1672. Dryden refers to the popularity of the visiting Company and the size and colour of their playbills.

> 'A brisk French Troop is grown your dear delight
> Who with broad bloody Bills call you each day
> To laugh and break your Buttons at their play.'

So, by the end of the 17th century it appears that a few larger bills or 'Great Bills' with the new red lettering were being produced for London theatres. in addition to the smaller, black-lettered bills.

Despite an order made in June 1700 by the Mayor and Aldermen of the City of London forbidding playhouse bills to be placarded in any part of the City or Liberties since they considered them likely to give encouragement to 'vice and prophaneness', bill-posting soon became general again. By this time theatre managers also inserted notices of their plays in the daily newspapers that had recently begun to be printed, but the bills were still a necessary form of advertisement. The red-lettered bills attracted more attention than the smaller black ones, as noted by the beau in a prologue to a play by Motteux, first performed at the Haymarket Theatre, 1706:

> 'Put out Red-letter'd Bills, and raise your Price
> You'll lure a select Audience in a trice.'

The red lettering was certainly more expensive than the black, as shown by the Drury Lane expense vouchers for 1712-16 when red bills cost fifteen shillings daily, and the black bills, ten shillings.

Gradually, more information about the plays, including occasionally the name of the author, began to appear on both sizes of bill. In the early 18th century it seems that the Great Bill was printed after the smaller bill, and was therefore the most up to date and detailed. The earliest playbill in the Theatre Museum, of the smaller size, notes that the performance of *Rule A Wife and Have A Wife*, Drury Lane 1718, will include 'Entertainments of Singing and Dancing, as will be Express'd in the Great Bille.' It is also surmounted by a royal crest, the earliest pictorial element on a playbill, which the printer added with a woodcut.

Both sizes of bill were posted up daily outside the theatres and at recognised places throughout London. As Theophilus Cibber stated in The Daily Advertiser, October 1744, plays at his theatre would be advertised 'in the Daily Post, the Daily Advertiser and the General Advertiser . . . the large Play-Bills and Hand Play Bills will be posted and delivered on the days of the performance only.'

The smaller bills were also available outside the theatres before the performance, but the previous custom of their free distribution was curtailed in the 18th century when the orange-sellers also sold the play-bills.

The Great Bill is the most immediate ancestor of the theatre poster as we know it. For the performance of *Cymbeline* at Covent Garden, 5 May 1779, the Theatre Museum possesses both the smaller and the larger bills. Printed in alternate lines of red and black type, the large bill (see plate 1) is more than four times the size of its smaller counterpart which is printed only in black. For the earlier Great Bills, the letterpress printers had no special typefaces, but chose the largest print they had in stock. In 1765 however, a printer called Thomas Cotterell had issued specimens of a special typeface for large posters called the 12-line Pica letter, and this is the typeface we see used in this poster of 1779.

By this date both bills give identical information; that the performance is a Benefit to take place at Covent Garden Theatre, and that it is a tragedy, although the author is not credited. They give the date, and the year of performance, list the cast with all the names of the actors in equal size of typeface, give notice of the Masquerade Dance and Song at the end of Act II, and the title and the cast of the Afterpiece. A note is added about ticket purchase, and they end with the programme for the following evening, although no mention is made of the time that the performance will begin.

Early in the 18th century, playbills had not given a cast list, but as this became customary, problems arose from performers who felt that their names should feature in the largest typeface. Prompters, whose job it was to write the playbills for the printers, found that it was all too easy to make enemies in the cast because of this task. One prompter, John Chetwood, wrote in 1794 complaining that recently:

> 'I have found it very difficult to please some ladies as well as gentlemen because I could not find letters large enough to please them; and some were so fond of elbow room that they would have shoved everyone out but themselves.'

The situation had apparently become so difficult by 1757 when Kemble was appointed Manager of Drury Lane Theatre that he insisted on all performers being listed on the bills in order of appearance, while at Covent Garden Theatre 'the actors are nominated according to their rank in the theatre, and in the new pieces, according to salary.' (Monthly Mirror 1799). It is with this equality of typeface that we see the cast list appear for *Cymbeline* on the Great Bill of 1779.

In the first few years of the 19th century the small playbills and handbills produced by theatres differed little from those of the previous fifty years. But over the next thirty years, developments in printing techniques encouraged change in the appearance of playbills which grew in size and abundance. The first commercially viable paper-making machine was set up in England in 1805, and typefounders introduced an increasing variety of display typefaces after the Fat Face appeared in 1803, and the Egyptian in 1817. New iron printing-presses, such as the Columbian and the Albion were used from the 1820s, which could print the new denser typefaces more successfully than the previous wooden presses. The increase in the number of theatres made managers more anxious to catch the attention of the public with large, boldly printed bills, promising wondrous entertainments with spectacular scenery and effects, music and dance. The managers of Astley's Circus in London particularly appreciated the possibilities afforded by the new typefaces and cheaper paper. Their playbills increased in size greatly between 1800 and 1833, and in addition to their large letterpress bills measuring $30'' \times 9\frac{1}{4}''$, they also produced posters, such as that for *The Siege of Troy* (see plate 2).

This Astley's poster, for the evening of 29 April 1833, features a magnificent woodcut of a gigantic Trojan horse, towering above the tiny figure of a soldier at his hooves. Such an image could hardly fail to attract attention, and an illiterate could ask for the text to be read to him when his interest had been aroused by the picture. In *Nicholas Nickelby*, the novel written by Charles Dickens in 1838, we read about the importance of illustrated bills when the theatre manager Mr. Crummles asks Nicholas to help him produce playbills. A play that Crummles is about to produce will feature a real pump and two washing tubs on stage. Crummles asks Nicholas if he is an artist and could draw them for the bills:

> 'That is not one of my accomplishments' rejoined Nicholas 'Ah! Then it can't be helped' said the manager 'If you had been we might have had a large woodcut of the last scene for the posters, showing the whole depth of the stage, with the pump and tubs in the middle.'

Dickens also tells us how the playbills were delivered and posted, and mentions the fact that the plays were still announced orally:

> 'The crier was sent round in the morning to proclaim the entertainments with the sound of bell in all the thoroughfares; and extra bills of three feet long by nine inches wide were dispersed in all directions; flung down all the areas, thrust under all the knockers, and developed in all the shops. They were placarded too, though not with complete success; for an illiterate person having undertaken this office during the indisposition of the regular bill-sticker, a part were posted sideways, and the remainder upside-down.'

Posting bills upside-down seems to have been a common problem, and hence another virtue of the illustrated bill was that the sticker was more likely to appreciate the correct position of the poster with a picture to assist him!

By the middle of the 19th century, woodcut or wood-engraved images were a popular feature of all sizes of posters and playbills, and a greater variety of coloured inks and papers were being used. The new letter-forms available to the printer were being designed with increasing inventiveness, and were combined flamboyantly on posters and playbills. The lettering for the word 'Masquerade' on the Vauxhall Gardens poster, 8 September 1859, (plate 3), is an example of virtuoso elaborate design in which printers revelled. The three dimensional letters are set at an angle, incorporating engraved images of popular theatrical characters on the letter forms. The poster for *Caste* at the Prince of Wales Theatre, 6 April 1861 (plate 4) is headed with a wood-engraved Prince of Wales feathers, while the title of the play stands out from the surrounding blue type in bold, black ink. Letter-forms cut in two or more units were available, allowing the printer to use combinations of colour and to achieve the popular 3-dimensional effect. This is used in the name 'Rubini' on the Egyptian Hall poster of c.1869 (plate 5), and on the Drury Lane pantomime poster for December 1871 (plate 6). But perhaps the most important advance in printing techniques in the first half of the 19th century to affect poster production was the development of colour lithography. This new technique effected the change from the woodcut and wood engraved illustrated playbills to the large, brightly coloured lithographic posters familiar to all by the end of the century.

Lithography was a printing method that had been invented as early as 1798 by Senefelder in Germany, and introduced in England about 1800. But it was not until Rudolf Ackermann and Charles Hullmandel established lithographic presses in London, c.1818, after visiting Munich, that printers in England began to look seriously at its possibilities for producing small coloured prints and music-sheet cover illustrations. Lithography was not a relief method of printing like woodcut or letterpress, but one which printed from a dampened slab of flat limestone on which the image was drawn with a greasy crayon. Each colour needed a separate printing, and although quicker and cheaper than copper engraving, it was at first much slower and more expensive than letterpress. The gradual introduction of powered lithographic machines after 1851 encouraged its use, but it was not until the 1860s that theatre managers began to invest in this new medium to advertise their performances.

The posters for *Arrah-Na-Pogue* at the Princess's Theatre, March 1865, (plate 7), and for Black Eye'd Susan at the New Royalty Theatre

December 1866, (plate 8), are examples of the new chromolithographic poster. They are smaller than the previous letterpress and woodcut posters, but far more subtle and delicate than any form of advertising seen hitherto for the theatre. Both are by artists who were well known for their colour lithograph illustrations for sheet music, and it was probably the attractiveness of these illustrated covers that influenced the production of the early chromolithographic posters. The poster advertising *Blue Beard* at Covent Garden Theatre, 26 December 1871, (plate 9), is another effective early chromolithographic poster, featuring in shades of blue the devilish hirsute face of Bluebeard, winking at the onlooker. This was still however a relatively expensive medium for larger images, and theatres could only occasionally afford the process until it became cheaper later in the century.

None of these posters gives detailed information about the plays, and it was the introduction of the theatre programme that had finally liberated the theatre poster. Until the late 1850s many theatres issued only a large playbill which had to serve the dual function of playbill and poster. But when managements realised how unwieldy the playbill had become, besmirching the patron with printer's ink, smaller programmes were introduced. This meant that much of the information necessary in the programme could be omitted from the poster, and gradually the image began to assume supreme importance on theatre posters. Another contributory factor to the issue of posters and programmes instead of only playbills, was the change from nightly differing entertainments to productions that were mounted at a theatre for a 'run', as they are today.

The new emphasis on the pictorial element in posters encouraged establishment artists to turn their attention to poster design, and in 1871 an Associate of the Royal Academy produced a poster for the Olympic Theatre. Frederick Walker's poster for the melodrama *The Woman In White* bestowed an important new status on poster design. Walker himself wrote prophetically:

'I am impressed on doing all I can with an attempt at what I consider might develop into a most important branch of art.'

Walker's poster was a large woodcut illustration, but as high-speed lithographic presses were developed that could reproduce large posters in quantity, every theatre wanted chromolithographic posters to attract patrons. In France in the 1880s and '90s the posters of Manet, Chéret and Lautrec were attracting attention, while in England hoardings were soon plastered with lithographic posters of various standards of design. Some printing firms, such as David Allen and Sons of Belfast, Manchester and London, finding the coloured posters so popular with theatre managers, issued series of 'stock' posters that could fit many productions. They could have offered an all-purpose 'domestic drama' poster, or a melodrama poster, on which the correct play title was overprinted. The posters for *Human Nature* at Drury Lane Theatre, September 1885, (plate 10), and *Hearts Are Trumps*, Drury Lane, September 1899, (plate 11), appear to be this type of stock poster. It would seem difficult to match the pictorial representation of the *Hearts Are Trumps* poster on stage, but as N. L. Parker wrote in 1882 about such 'pictorial representations in vivid colours of exciting events in the play':

> 'Accuracy is scarcely a strong point with these 'posters' for when seen on stage, the crowds are not so fierce, the shipwrecks a little less awful, whilst the cliff down which the hero descends in immaculate garb (without crumpling his collar) proves at least a hundred foot lower than the cliff at which the street-boys gaze, full of wonder and admiration.'

Revelling in the newly available method of colour lithography, those responsible for publicity were at first keen to depict scenes from their plays or entertainments on their posters. Magic and circus acts were colourful subjects for colourful posters, and the magic poster, c.1880 (plate 12) features a levitation act by John Nevil Maskelyne, one of Maskelyne's 'Modern Miracles' performed at the Egyptian Hall, dubbed 'England's Home of Mystery'. The poster used for F. W. Wyllie's tours during the late 19th century (plate 13) combines lithograph and letterpress. Four acts are depicted within decorative borders, surmounted by clown and animal heads; an energetic scene of horsemanship and acrobatics fills the lower part of the poster, while a white-faced clown peers through the 'C' of 'Circus' at the top.

When 'The Poster' magazine first appeared in 1898, the author of an article on pantomine posters declared:

> 'Until recently, almost nothing artistic was born of the annual pantomine (poster design) competition. The theatrical manager was content to incite the colour printer's hack to a more than unusually riotous orgy, and the public did not murmur at the abominable result. If the bill was big enough, and of sufficiently lurid colour, it was deemed perfectly to fulfil its purpose. Nor indeed was novelty ever thought of: the stock printing of 1885 was voted appropriate for a production of ten years later. Even when musical comedies and the like were heralded with some approach to good taste and distinction, the pantomime remained high and dry on its island of vulgarity.'

The poster for *Jack and the Beanstalk* at Drury Lane, December 1899, falls into the category of riotously coloured poster, although most people today would enjoy its vivid representation of an army being released from the body of the dead giant (plate 14). It is, however, very different from the posters of Dudley Hardy and John Hassall which *The Poster* magazine praised for their simplicity of line and colour.

Dudley Hardy (1867-1922) was employed by the innovative manager of the Savoy Theatre, Richard D'Oyly Carte, to design posters for productions at his theatre. Perhaps the most stunning poster Hardy created for him was that for the first revival of *The Yeoman of the Guard*, May 1897 (plate 15). *The Poster* magazine of 1899 praised the yellow, crimson and sage green colour scheme, but declared that:

> 'The masked headsman with his formidable axe and block is undoubtedly gruesome, and it may be questioned whether an opera which, in spite of occasional lapses into genuine pathos, is on the whole so light and amusing, was altogether properly announced by so repellant a design.'

In fact, Richard D'Oyly Carte was commissioning such successful posters in the 1880s, at a time when poster design was being newly appreciated as an art form, that he was bedevilled by collectors removing them from their sites. They removed them at night, with the aid of a damp sponge, and Carte was driven to add on some of his posters the words:

> 'This poster is the property of Mr., R.D'Oyly Carte, London, and any person selling, or receiving same is liable to prosecution.'

This was quite a different problem from that of half a century earlier when managers complained of their bills being posted upside-down, or being immediately covered by the poster of a rival theatre, as we see happening on the cover illustration of a poster hoarding in 1840, painted by John Parry.

Dudley Hardy had begun his career training to be a painter, studying in Dusseldorf, Antwerp and Paris, but it was as a poster artist that he achieved greatest acclaim. His paintings were exhibited at the Royal Academy of Art in 1885, 1886 and 1889, and he could not agree with those artists who felt it degrading to exhibit on poster hoardings as well as on the walls of the Royal Academy. His thoughts on the subject were quoted in 'The Poster', December 1899:

> 'My idea is that an advertisement, both from the artistic and commercial point of view, should be as simple and striking as possible; very little background, very little detail, a bold, striking line which will arrest the eye of the passer-by. There is nothing, surely, derogatory to an artist in that, is there? Why he should confine his attention to painting pictures for a frame I cannot imagine; he can have no finer canvas than that of the walls of London, and I am quite sure he cannot have a more critical audience than that of the London streets.'

Hardy's early posters reveal his admiration of the French poster artist Jules Chéret (1836-1933), who had come to London in 1856 to study the modernised version of the machinery invented by

Senefelder for processing colour lithography. Hardy would have seen Chéret's exuberant posters on the hoardings in Paris, advertising everything from medicines to masked balls. The frothy ladies on Chéret's posters twirled and sang, and the poster advertising the Minstrels Parisiens at the Palace Theatre, November 1895, (plate 16), shows how Chéret's influence danced its way effortlessly across the Channel.

But while Hardy's Gaiety Girl and Yellow Girl posters showed his debt to Chéret, his poster for *The Yeomen of the Guard* demonstrates his belief that posters should be simple, with very little background, and 'a bold, striking line which will arrest the eye of the passer-by.' This quality is also seen in the poster for *The Only Way*, Lyceum, February 1899 (plate 17), designed by Hardy's contemporary, John Hassall. Also trained as a painter in Antwerp and Paris, Hassall too became convinced by the power of simple, two-dimensional poster art. The example of the Japanese woodcut with its dramatic viewpoints and broad, unshaded areas of colour, had influenced the work of many artists who designed posters, including Toulouse Lautrec in France and Aubrey Beardsley in England. Hassall's admiration for Japanese prints is evident from his use of dramatic horizontal and vertical lines in the scaffolding, combined with the stark white area of the hero's coat. The image is uncompromising. The blades of the weapons wielded by the onlookers point unrelentingly to the scaffold. The threatening sky emphasises the dark mood, as does the glowering crimson setting sun behind the headsman in Hardy's *Yeoman* poster.

In a less dramatic way, the poster for *The Geisha*, Daly's Theatre, 1896, (plate 18), again demonstrates the influence of the Japanese print. The Geisha stands like a cut-out doll, the pierced shape of the curving hand-rail behind her contrasting with the flat, dark area of her kimono. This poster, advertising a play about a Japanese subject, even includes integrated oriental-style lettering which is however somewhat spoiled by the unsympathetic overprinting of 'The Spa Theatre, Scarborough.'

Excellence is never the rule, and 'hack' poster design existed alongside the specially commissioned well-designed posters as it does today. In 1900, David Allen and Sons offered over 700 examples of their 'off the peg' lithographic posters for theatrical performances offering: 'such a wide range and variety of subjects that suitable pictorials for almost any piece are practically certain to be found among our stock.' They also produced letterpress slips, printed from type to imitate lithography, for pasting on top of posters to give the appropriate copy 'in such an artistic manner' as to appear to have been printed with the picture. Nevertheless, the last two decades of the 19th century saw major developments in poster art. In France, Chéret was awarded the 'Légion d'Honneur' in 1899 for 'creating a new branch of art, by applying art to commercial and industrial painting.' The same year saw exhibitions on the history of the poster, and of Chéret posters in Paris. Promoters of events and products on both sides of the Channel realised the value of good advertisements, and vied with each other for the best sites for their posters. Hoardings with specified rates for poster advertising were established, although that never hindered illegal billposting, and sandwich-board men were hired to carry posters like Boardie Willie in Whitby (see illustration on back cover). 'The Poster' magazine, June 1898, complimented the Advertising Manager of the Palace Theatre in London for being the first to commission an artistic 'bus bill, since, they stated: 'hitherto we have had only letterpress travelling the streets'. An example of a letterpress poster on a London 'bus is seen in Concanen's illustrated cover for the music sheet *A Run For the Bus* of 1884 (see ill. on page 10). There was still an abundance of letterpress bills at the end of the century, however, as there is today, and well-designed posters such as those for *A Greek Slave*, Daly's 1898 (plate 19), and *Dr. Nikola*, Fulham Grand, June 1902 (plate 20), must surely have stood out from their mediocre companions on the hoardings, each featuring a compelling image of a central character.

Between 1900 and 1914 advances were made in

A Run For The Bus by T. S. Lonsdale & Louis Raynal.
Music sheet cover illustration. Colour lithograph by Alfred Concanen,
1884. CT.11081.

the technology of colour printing which aided the mass production of posters and prints. The cumbersome lithographic stone was replaced by grained zinc or aluminium plates; the four-colour lithographic system was perfected whereby all colours could be produced by the overprinting of a magenta colour, a blue, a yellow and a black; and in America the basic principles of 'offset' lithographic printing were devised. In 'offset' the image is transferred from an inked lithographic plate attached to a roller on to a rubber roller which in turn prints on the paper. This meant that the printer could work from designs and lettering drawn the correct way round, instead of from a reversed image which was necessary when the print was taken directly from the lithographic stone. The introduction of offset lithography encouraged the development of photographic lithography (or 'photolithography') whereby the image on the lithographic plate is made from a half-tone photograph. This is the technique used for the poster of May Moore Duprez, printed c.1912 (plate 21).

May Moore Duprez—'The Jolly Little Dutch Girl, cute and sassy comedienne' (1881-1946), needed her own image to be the main feature of her poster since it advertised her act with which she toured. Thus the name of the relevant theatre or Music Hall would have been overprinted. An American, specialising in an impersonation of a clog-dancing Dutch girl, May Moore Duprez first appeared in London in 1901, doing her 'solo cake walk song and dance act' at the New Cross Empire, and at the Oxford and Tivoli Music Halls.

Another important advance in the technology of colour printing in the early 20th century was the introduction of silkscreen printing. The first patent for this in England was granted in 1907 to Samuel Simon in Manchester who used a stopping-out liquid to paint the negative image on to a mesh of bolting silk stretched on to a wooden frame. By pouring ink on the frame and forcing it through the mesh, the 'positive' areas left un-stopped were thus printed. This basic technique was further developed in the United States, where the first photographic silkscreen stencil was produced. Highly mechanised silkscreen printing and offset litho are two of the major processes used in poster production today.

Perversely, as methods of poster production became more sophisticated in the early years of the century, so the general standard of posters seems to have declined. A contributory factor in this may have been the diminishing involvement of the artist in the actual poster production due to the more complex printing processes. Nevertheless, when competent artists or designers with a feel for dramatic illustration were commissioned, the results could be stunning, as for example the posters for *Macbeth*, His Majesty's Theatre 1911 (plate 22), and *A Midsummer Night's Dream*, Savoy Theatre 1914 (plate 23). The *Macbeth* poster, by the French illustrator, painter and designer Edmund Dulac (1882-1953) shows a move away from the earlier two-dimensional style characterised by the posters of Hardy and Hassall. Dulac's *Macbeth* image is that of an illustrator rather than a poster artist, but effective and mysterious from its unusual viewpoint and subtle colouring. Macbeth's back is turned towards the onlooker who sees only the faces of the two witches illuminated by the smoke of their cauldron. The hands of the witch in the foreground, and the gaze of Macbeth, lead to the white smoke which is the focal point of the poster, contrasting with the sombre surrounding blues and blacks. In the Savoy poster the red figure of Puck is the focal point, and the artist cleverly combines both two and three-dimensional figure representation, dividing the areas of the poster by blue whiplash curves. This striking and unusual image was a remarkable poster for an equally remarkable production by the actor and producer Harley Granville Barker.

While the posters for *Macbeth* and *A Midsummer Night's Dream* each reflect the atmosphere of the production, the poster by G. K Benda for *The Flowers of Allah*, part of the review *Eightpence A Mile* at the Alhambra Theatre, 1913 (plate 24), faithfully depicts the striking scenery designed by Ronsin, and the costumes by Poiret. This luminous poster features a stylised dancer in an oriental setting, the effect reminiscent of a Persian miniature. Another stylised figure features in H. M. Brock's poster for the D'Oyly Carte Company's production of *Patience*, Princes Theatre 1919 (plate 25). Like his father Richard D'Oyly Carte who commissioned Dudley Hardy's *Yeomen* poster, Rupert D'Oyly Carte realised the value of eye-catching poster design. Here the poet Bunthorne is seen adoring a lily, and being adored by three of his retinue of twenty love-sick maidens. The style is reminiscent of that of Hardy thirty years previously—a plain background against which is set a tableau of clearly outlined figures. Printed without any reference to a theatre, this poster would have been used while the Company was in London and on tour, the name of the appropriate theatre being overprinted.

The poster advertising the act of the illusionist The Great Barrie (plate 26) was another 1920s touring poster, again with a blank space for the name of the relevant theatre. The poster artist has framed his image within the curtains and footlights, and has tried to make the lettering of: 'The Great Barrie Originator' appear as if printed on the curtains at the back of the stage. For the sake of the poster we can see through the box to the manacled girl being sawn in half, and the static figures are decidedly humorous. Drama, and not humour was probably the intention of the artist, but the resulting poster is a good example of popular poster art in the tradition of the 19th-century Rubini and Egyptian Hall posters (plates 5 & 12).

Although similar in date, a complete contrast to the previous poster is George Sheringham's colour lithograph advertising *The Duenna* at the Lyric Theatre, Hammersmith, October 1924 (plate 27). George Sheringham (1884-1937) was trained as a painter in London and Paris, but soon turned his attention to interior decoration, commercial and theatre design. He designed posters advertising the London Underground in 1924, and these were praised by the Design and Industries Association who aimed to improve the standard of art and lettering in advertising. Sheringham's theatrical posters often made use of his own costume designs for productions, as in this poster for *The Duenna*, and it is a tribute to the simplicity and clarity of his designs that they could bear the enlargement necessary for a poster. Sheringham designed all the sets and costumes for this production of Sheridan's comic opera, and worked successfully on many other productions for Nigel Playfair's Lyric Theatre in Hammersmith.

Like Sheringham's poster for *The Duenna*, that for *The Old Adam* (plate 28) includes large, simple lettering, but its subject is the theme of the play instead of one of its costume designs. *The Old Adam*, by Cicely Hamilton, was produced by Barry Jones at the Kingsway Theatre, November 1925. A 'thoughtful comedy', with a serious message about the futility of war, the play features a scientist who discovers a ray that will prevent war by paralysing every mechanical device within a radius of several hundred miles. Sadly, this does not discourage the belligerent nations involved, who simply bring warfare to its most primitive state, fighting with fishing boats and fists instead of with aeroplanes and rifles. The artist J. Campbell Owen has captured the spirit of the play, showing on the poster the moment when the scientist operates his invention which radiates the immobilising beams. The rounded, geometric forms and the fragmented composition recall Vorticist paintings of ten years earlier, and the startling monochrome image makes an eye-catching and effective advertisement for a well-received play.

Two circus posters of 1928, for Carmo's Circus and Menagerie, (plate 29), and Bertram Mills' Circus (plate 30), are examples of colourful poster art calculated to attract large audiences to a very popular form of entertainment. Both are colour lithographs, and while the Carmo poster illustrates the menagerie of animals as if it were a glorious public Noah's Ark, that for Bertram Mills' circus concentrates on the figure of a white-faced clown. Mills was particularly astute about good publicity and for many years most of his posters were designed by Leon Crossley and produced by the printing firm of W. E. Berry Ltd., in Bradford, who still produce circus posters today. Crossley would sketch acts during rehearsals and produce very honest representations of the performances on his posters. Crossley's clown has an irresistible charm, with his big grin, his bow tie, tuba, a duck-filled carpet bag and balloon!

For posters advertising their circus, Bertram Mills and his sons insisted on a variety of original poster designs for each season, but on the whole the standard of pictorial posters began to decline in the 1930s. Greater emphasis was put on mainly typographical posters, despite some excellent posters such as those commissioned by London Transport. Photographic images were used increasingly in poster design, and cinema posters relied heavily on photographs of popular 'stars'. When most London theatres were closed during the Second World War, posters were a major propaganda tool, but they were not vital for conscription purposes as they had been in the Great War, and less effective designs were produced. When the theatres reopened, paper was still scarce and posters were small, giving the basic necessary information.

The advent of television in the 1950s, bringing realistic images into the home, further encouraged photographic representation on theatre posters. Many posters of the 1950s were still, however, purely typographic, as those for the Royal Court Theatre which used the same format as that for *Look Back In Anger*, October 1957 (plate 31) for all its posters and programme covers in 1957 and 1958. It was not until the early 1960s that imaginative poster design began to flourish again generally, fostered by the Pop Art movement which used screenprinting extensively for colourful posters. 'Flower-power' images and colours burgeoned; poster shops blossomed, and posters became a popular form of wall decoration for student rooms and fashionable homes alike. Liberation of colours in the '60s artwork and fashion heralded the liberation of theatres, and in 1968 the Theatres Act abolished stage censorship in Great Britain. *Hair*, the American musical which might previously have offended the Lord Chamberlain's officials, was produced at the Shaftesbury Theatre in September 1968. The poster reflects the mystical, dream-like atmosphere of the show. 'The Age of Aquarius' was here. *Hair* was on the London stage. The mirror image of two heads with 'Afro-style' hair announced the musical from the hoardings in garish red, yellow and green, printed by the offset litho process (plate 32).

The abolition of stage censorship also meant that plays by Joe Orton (1933-1967) could be performed in public. *What The Butler Saw*, a farce set in a psychiatric clinic, was first produced in Brighton in 1969, and the poster for the Royal Court revival of 1975 features photo-collage images as irreverent as the play itself. This technique deliberately parodies Orton's own predilection for collage which resulted in a six month prison sentence after he and his friend Kenneth Halliwell once defaced library books with collage. In this poster a god-like figure surrounded by the title of the play flies with Concorde, while below a policeman stands on bare buttocks; Orton's own face is seen, and the Queen and Winston Churchill stare out over naked figures, nuns and a television set (plate 33).

A masked pig with female breasts and well-manicured hands, smoking a pipe and drinking a bottle of beer is another startling image, this time for a poster for *Bartholomew Fair*. Designed by Stephen Games for the Arts Theatre, Cambridge, March 1977 (plate 34), this image symbolises the general debauchery of an Elizabethan Fair, and belies the description of Ben Jonson's play as a 'discrete comedie'. The best posters immediately catch the attention of the passer-by and whether the reaction caused by this poster is of revulsion or humour, it has certainly succeeded in this aim.

Ginni Moo-Young's silkscreen poster for the Royal Shakespeare Company's production of *All's Well That Ends Well*, 1982, is also eye-catching in a very different, lyrical way. Printed in dark blue, light blue and cream, the swirling patterns of the skirt in the foreground lead the eye to the heads of the dancing couple and the white shape of the pierced arch above (plate 35). Both romantic and nostalgic, this art-nouveau inspired poster concentrates totally on the image and the title of this play and was produced purely for sale in the RSC's theatres in Stratford and the Barbican. As the Director of this production, Trevor Nunn, said:

> This poster had to break the news to an unsuspecting world that the production of *Alls Well That Ends Well* was going to take place in the society of the 'Belle Epoque', and that since among other things the play challenges the traditional social roles of men and women. the ritual and sexuality of the dance was to be an important visual image in the staging.
> RSC posters must be informative, decorative and evocative, and as souvenirs they must capture the essence of the production they advertise; but have little or nothing to do with selling.

BY PARTICULAR DESIRE
For the Benefit of Mr. REDDISH.
Theatre-Royal, Covent-Garden,
This present Wednesday, MAY 5, 1779,
Will be presented a Tragedy, call'd
CYMBELINE.
Posthumus by Mr. REDDISH,
(Being his SECOND APPEARANCE this Season)
Cloten by Mr. LEE LEWES,
Cymbeline by Mr. L'ESTRANGE,
Pisanio by Mr. HULL,
Bellarius by Mr. CLARKE,
Guiderius by Mr. WROUGHTON,
Arviragus by Mr. WHITFIELD,
Caius Lucius, Mr. FEARON, Philario, Mr. BOOTH,
And Jachimo by Mr. SMITH,
[From the THEATRE-ROYAL in DRURY-LANE]
Queen by Mrs. JACKSON,
And Imogen by Mrs. BULKLEY.
End of Act II. a Masquerade Dance, and a Song by Mrs. MORTON.
To which will be added a FARCE, call'd
Three Weeks After Marriage.
Sir Charles Racket by Mr. LEWIS,
Drugget by Mr. QUICK,
Lovelace, Mr. BOOTH, Woodley Mr THOMPSON,
Dimity by Mrs. GREEN,
Nancy, Mrs WHITFIELD, Mrs. Drugget, Mrs. PITT,
Lady Racket by Mrs. MATTOCKS.
" Tickets sold at the Doors will not be admitted."
To-morrow, a new Tragedy, [Never Performed] called
FATAL FALSHOOD.
With a PROLOGUE & EPILOGUE, and a New Musical Piece, [never performed] called
The CHELSEA PENSIONER.
With new Scenes, Dresses, and Decorations.

PLATE I *Cymbeline*. Poster for Covent Garden Theatre, 5 May 1779. Letterpress. S.1-1983. CT.11055.

PLATE 2   *The Siege of Troy*. Poster for Astley's Theatre, 29 April 1883. Woodcut and letterpress. S.2-1983. CT.11056.

PLATE 3 *A Masquerade*. Poster for Vauxhall Gardens, 8 September 1859. Letterpress. S.3-1983. CT.11057.

PLATE 4 *Caste*. Poster for Prince of Wales Theatre, 6 April 1861. Woodcut and letterpress. S.4-1983. CT.11058.

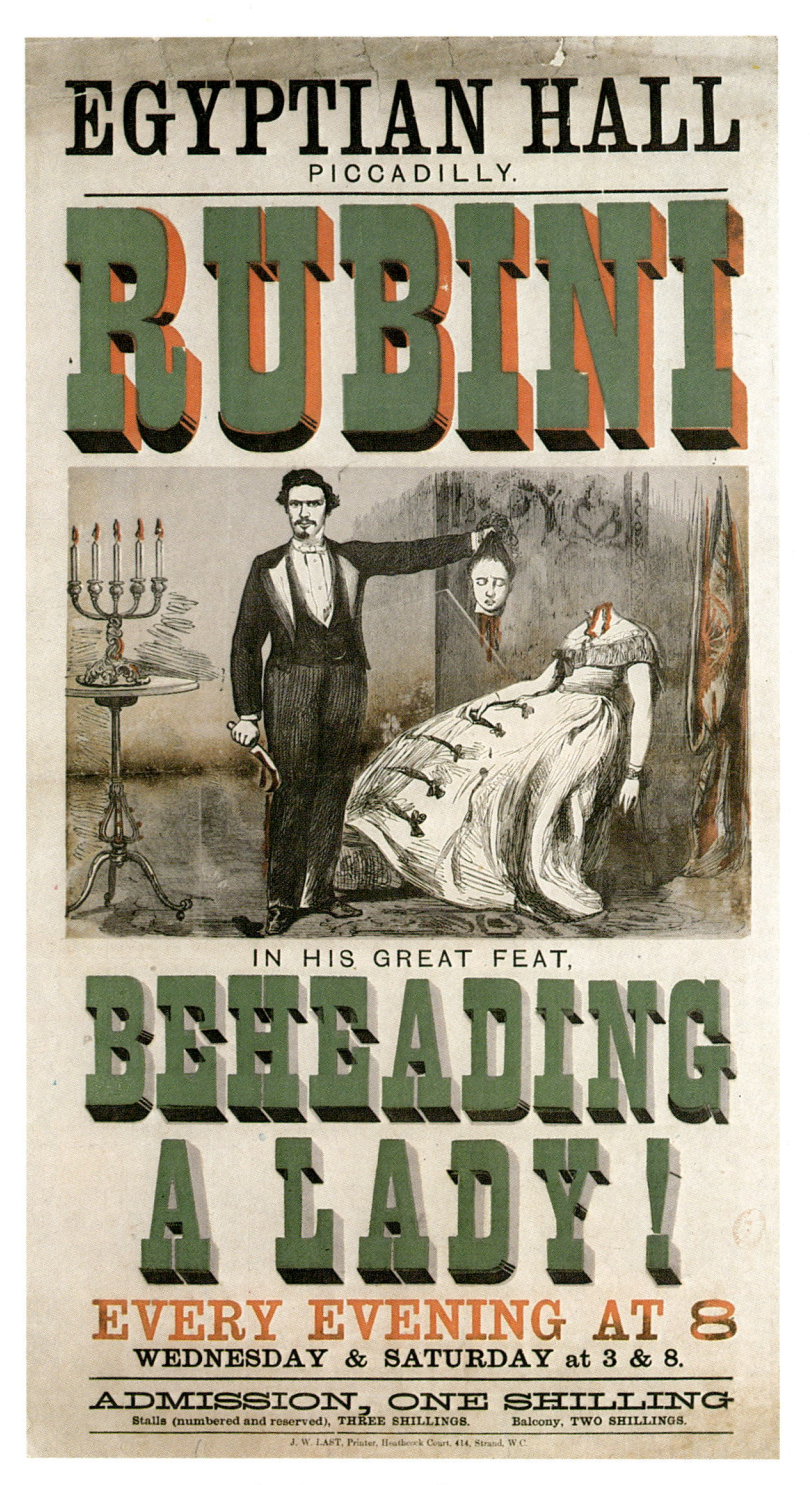

PLATE 5 *Rubini*. Poster for the Egyptian Hall, c.1869. Woodcut and letterpress. S.5-1983. CT.11059.

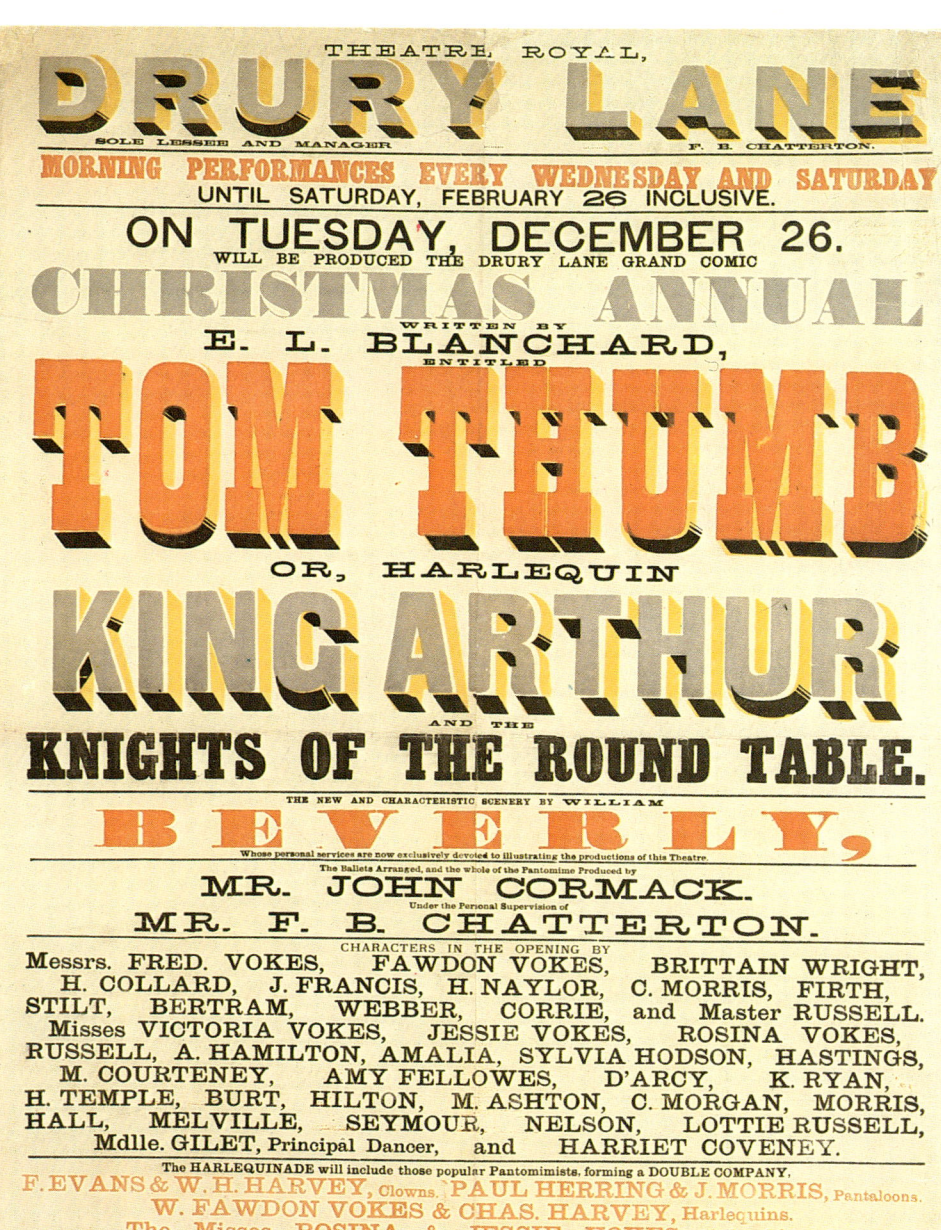

PLATE 6 *Tom Thumb, or, Harlequin King Arthur.* Poster for Drury Lane Theatre, December 1871. Letterpress. S.6-1983. CT.11060.

PLATE 7 *Arrah-Na-Pogue*. Poster for Princess's Theatre, March 1865. Colour lithograph. S.7-1983. CT.11061.

PLATE 8 *Black Eye'd Susan*. Poster for the New Royalty Theatre, December 1886.
Colour lithograph. S.8-1983. CT.11062.

PLATE 9 *Blue Beard*. Poster for Covent Garden Theatre, 26 December 1871. Colour lithograph. CT.10116.

PLATE 10 *Human Nature*. Poster for Drury Lane Theatre, September 1885. Colour lithograph. S.9-1983. CT.11063.

PLATE 11 *Hearts Are Trumps.* Poster for Drury Lane Theatre, September 1899.
Colour lithograph. S.10-1983. CT.10122.

PLATE 12 *Egyptian Hall.* Poster depicting a magic act by John Nevil Maskelyne, c.1880. S.11-1983. CT.10127.

PLATE 13 *F. W. Wyllie's Circus*. Touring poster, late 19th century. A. D. Hippisley Coxe Collection 2.53. CT.10153.

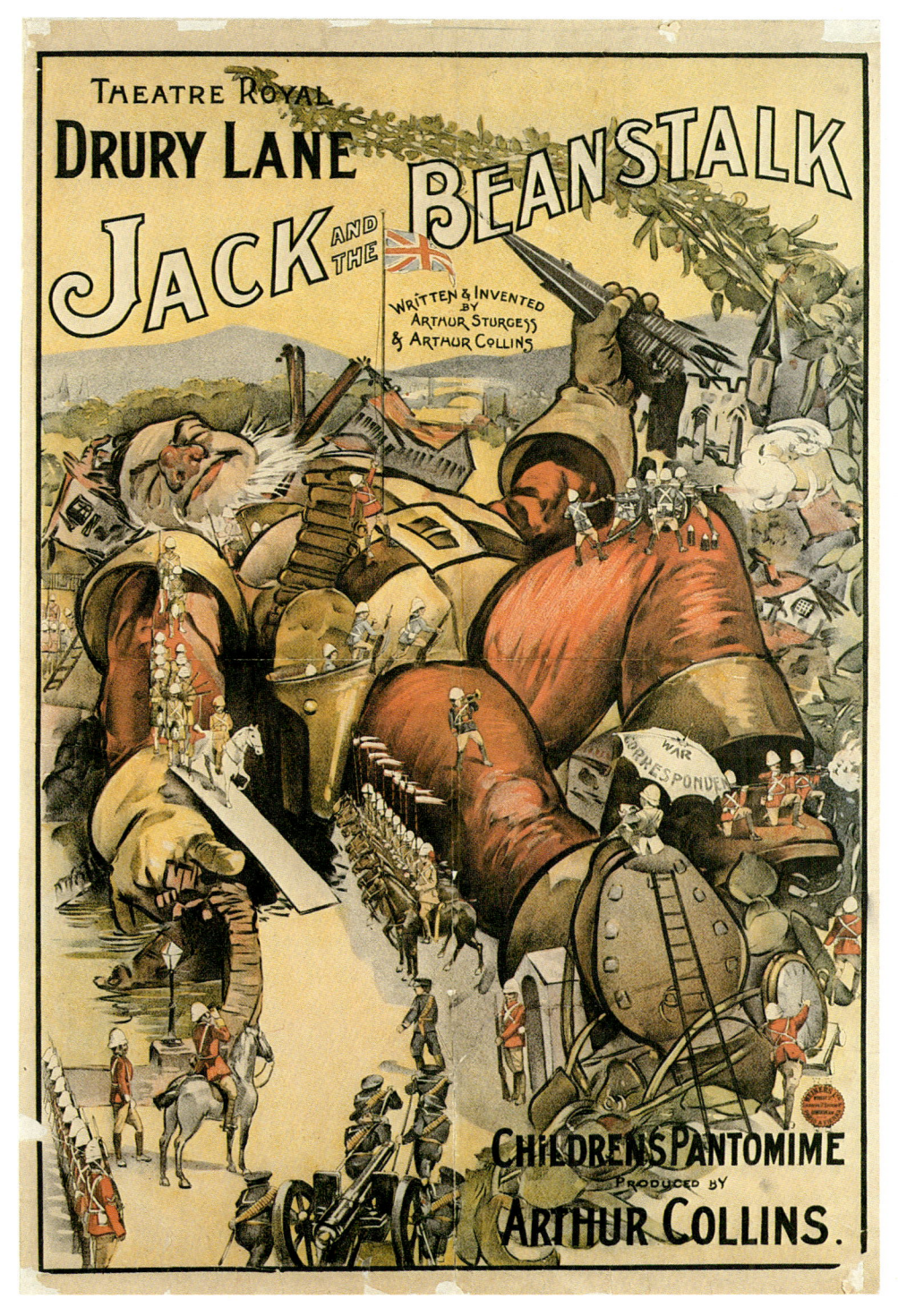

PLATE 14 *Jack and The Beanstalk*. Poster for Drury Lane Theatre, December 1899. Colour lithograph. S.12-1983. CT.11064.

PLATE 15 *The Yeomen of The Guard.* Poster for the Savoy Theatre, May 1897.
Colour lithograph. Designed by Dudley Hardy. S.13-1983. CT.11065.

PLATE 16 *Minstrels Parisiens*. Poster for the Palace Theatre of Varieties, November 1895. Colour lithograph. S.14-1983. CT.11066.

PLATE 17 *The Only Way*. Poster for the Lyceum Theatre, February 1899. Colour lithograph. Designed by John Hassall. S.15-1983. CT.4370.

PLATE 18 *The Geisha.* Poster for Daly's Theatre, 1896. Colour lithograph. S.16-1983. CT.11067.

PLATE 19 *A Greek Slave*. Poster for Daly's Theatre, 1898. Colour lithograph. S.17-1983. CT.11068.

PLATE 20 *Dr. Nikola*. Poster for Fulham Grand Theatre, June 1902. Colour lithograph. S.18-1983. CT.11082.

PLATE 21 *May Moore Duprez.* Poster for 'The Jolly Little Dutch Girl', c.1912. Photolithograph. S.32-1983. CT.11069.

PLATE 22 *Macbeth*. Poster for His Majesty's Theatre, 5 September 1911. Colour lithograph. Designed by Edmund Dulac. S.19-1983. CT.11070.

PLATE 23 *A Midsummer Night's Dream.* Poster for the Savoy Theatre, 6 February 1914. Colour lithograph. Designed by Graham Robertson. S.20-1983. CT.10125. Reproduced by courtesy of Hamish Hamilton.

PLATE 24. *Eightpence A Mile*. Poster for the Alhambra Theatre, 9 May 1913.
Colour lithograph. Designed by G. K. Benda. S.722-1982. CT.11072.

PLATE 25 *Patience*. Poster for the Princes Theatre, 24 November 1919. Colour lithograph. Designed by H. M. Brock. S.21-1983. CT.11071.

PLATE 26 *The Great Barrie.* Poster advertising a magician and illusionist, c.1920. Colour lithograph. S.444-1980. CT.10128.

PLATE 27 *The Duenna*. Poster for the Lyric Theatre, Hammersmith, 23 October 1924. Colour lithograph. Designed by George Sheringham. S.22-1983. CT.11073. Reproduced by courtesy of Penelope Turing.

PLATE 28 *The Old Adam*. Poster for the Kingsway Theatre, November 1925.
Lithograph. Designed by J. Campbell Owen. S.23-1983. CT.11074.

PLATE 29 *Great Carmo's Circus, Menagerie and Horse Show.* Poster for appearance in Margate, July 1928. Colour lithograph. S.30-1983. CT.11075

PLATE 30 *Bertram Mills Circus.* Poster for Olympia season, 1928. Colour lithograph. Designed by Leon Crossley. S.31-1983. CT.11076. Reproduced by courtesy of Leon Crossley.

44

Royal Court Theatre

Sloane Square S.W.1

Licensed by the London County Council to Alfred Esdaile

English Stage Company
Artistic Director George Devine

Clare Austin   Willoughby Gray   Alec McCowen
Gary Raymond   Anna Steele

October 28th to November 23rd

Four Weeks Only

LOOK BACK IN ANGER

by

John Osborne

Original Production by Tony Richardson
Directed by John Dexter
Setting: Alan Tagg   Music: Thomas Eastwood

All Seats bookable 5/-, 7/6, 10/6 and 15/-
Box Office SLOane 1745
Mon. to Fri. 7-30   Sat. 5 & 8-15   Mat. Wed. 2-30

PLATE 31 *Look Back In Anger*. Poster for the Royal Court Theatre, 28 October 1957. Offset and letterpress. S.24-1983. CT.11083. Reproduced by courtesy of the Royal Court Theatre.

PLATE 32   *Hair*. Poster for the Shaftesbury Theatre, 27 September 1968. Photolitho. S.25-1983. CT.11077.

PLATE 33 *What The Butler Saw*. Poster for the Royal Court Theatre, 1975. Photo-litho. Designed by Lindsay Anderson/Yves Simard. S.26-1983. CT.11078. Reproduced by courtesy of Lindsay Anderson.

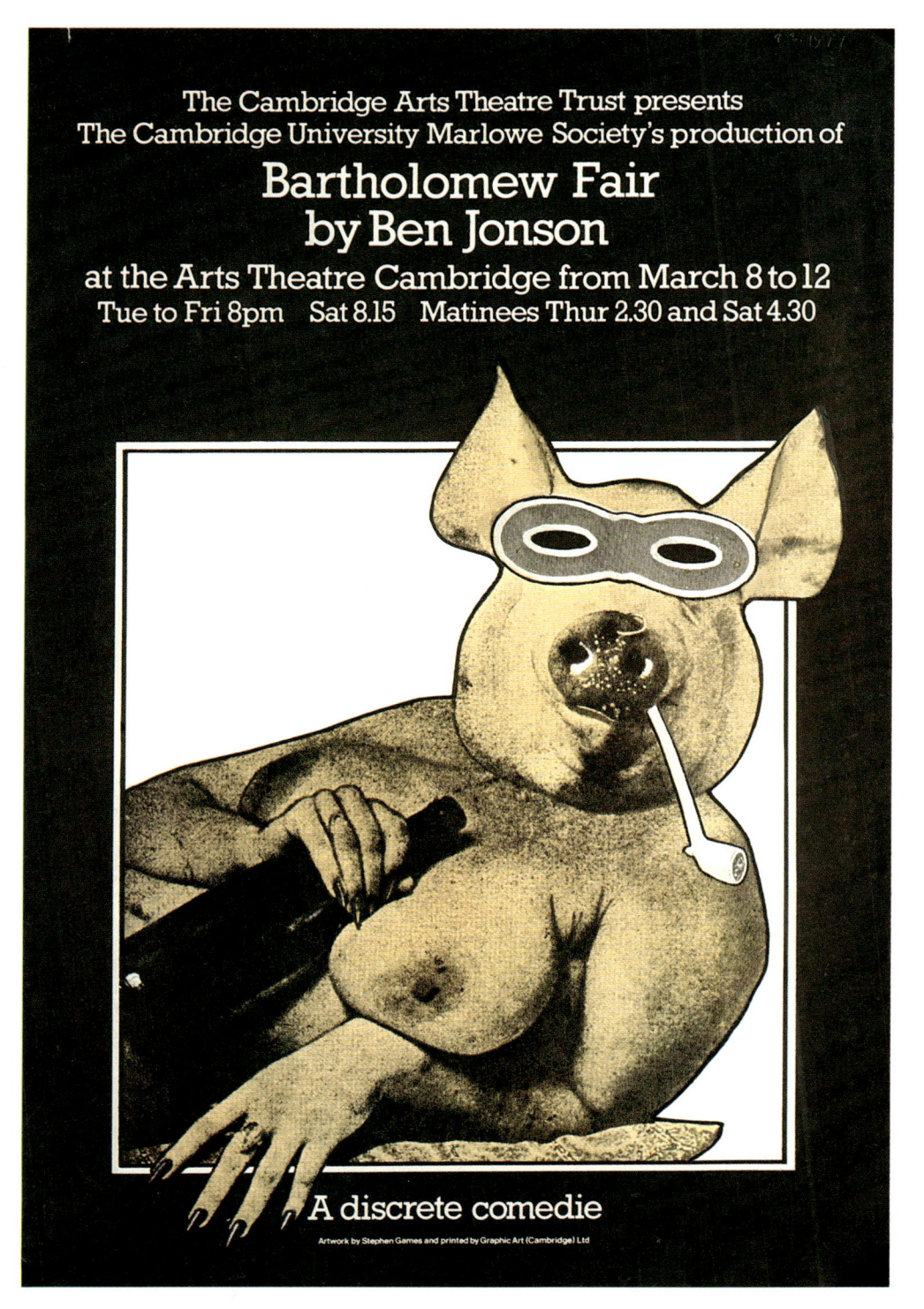

PLATE 34 *Bartholomew Fair*. Poster for the Arts Theatre, Cambridge, March 1977. Silk screen. Designed by Stephen Games. S.27-1983. CT.11079. Reproduced by courtesy of The Marlowe Society

PLATE 35. *All's Well That Ends Well.* Poster for the Royal Shakespeare Company, 1982. Silk screen. Designed by Ginni Moo-Young. S.28-1983. CT.11080. Reproduced by courtesy of Ginni Moo-Young.